Acclaim for Sherry Quan Lee's
Septuagenarian

In *Septuagenarian*, Sherry Quan Lee accepts her own invitation to look at life in retrospect, but with a new lens. Pulling from and expanding upon her previous body of work, she examines the version of herself that was writing at that time. Working as a therapist in racial identity development, I invite people to look at themselves in context. Seeing oneself in context decreases the judgment and shaming that comes from making lifetime decisions in childhood. Sherry's self-assessment is curious, assertive, open and unapologetic. She holds many versions of past selves, looking plainly at her training to pass as White and to squeeze into the tight, traditional roles of woman, wife and mother. And then she lifts the veil, showing us the pain of this training, the rage that followed captivity in ill-fitting boxes and the forward movement that inevitably follows forgiveness. The dignity and fire of her seventy-three-year old gaze taking in snapshots of those selves... straightens my spine and gives me a vision for myself traveling today into my future septuagenarian.

~ Lola Osunkoya, MA, LPCC

I've been reading Sherry Quan Lee's work for almost thirty years and her voice keeps getting stronger, more urgent, deeper. In *Septuagenarian*, she continues to write out of her past, "the Black/Chinese/girl passing for white," but the range of her voice is wider now, both inward and outward and it's anchored by a wisdom that can only be achieved through struggle and time. This is a significant, heartfelt work, one that will help readers to understand not only the author and her life, but also America itself--what we have been, what we are and, hopefully, what we might become.

~ David Mura, author of *A Stranger's Journey: Race, Identity & Narrative Craft in Writing*

Septuagenarian by Sherry Quan Lee is a book that answers, in many different ways, the question posed in one of the poems contained within: "What does surrender look like?" Surrender looks like passion, like the banishment of shame, like truth telling. The narrator is not afraid of death, but embraces the inseparability and magnitude of opposing forces: "The world is a large body of terror where good and evil coexist, and each of us is responsible." Quan Lee's bold language makes space for living within impossibilities. It is a book that maps, often with aching beauty, many of the author's passions, desires, grief and the circularity of life at seventy, "I have lost so many people over time, but at seventy long-term memory brings them back, both the wicked and the wise…story ends where it begins."

~ 신 선 영 辛善英 Sun Yung Shin,
author of *Unbearable Splendor*

Septuagenarian is a poignant retrospective covering seven decades of Sherry Quan Lee's life, culminating in 2020, the year of the COVID-19 pandemic. In this collection, which blends new work with poems published in her previous books, Quan Lee reckons with invisibility—a mixed-race woman who was raised white/ "a gray-haired specter" "the critics ignore." The pain and frustration caused by the pervasive, divisive effects of generational trauma on herself and her family are no longer obstacles, and love is no longer imagined—and the world at large explored.

~ Carolyn Holbrook, author of
Tell Me Your Names and I Will Testify

Sherry Quan Lee writes with a purity of intention. She has no interest in certain kinds of poetics that conceal, or only honor, adornment. She has her gaze on the long sweep of her personal history. She reflects on old wounds, key mistakes and certain joys. She pushes against clichéd thinking or feeling. She is hard on herself, in these poems, in ways few poets are. She honors the complicated narratives of race, of being female, of living a long life and works to discern the point of it all. I've read and taught Sherry Quan Lee's work for a very long time now and am grateful for this new collection.

~ Deborah Keenan, author of ten collections of poetry and a book of writing ideas, *from tiger to prayer*

In *Septuagenarian: love is what happens when I die*, Sherry Quan Lee writes courageously to understand herself and the world. She uses rich language and her skills as a storyteller to focus her sharp lens on what it means to have a complex, sometimes complicated identity: becoming invisible as she ages, a history of passing unseen, love and sex, grieving and celebration. She ruminates on history, which repeats itself in the current moment and widens her lens to look at the bigger, global picture to tell truths in poems that tenderly hold memory, time, rituals, trauma, mothering, fear of death and love in many forms. Her poems offer deeply personal, intimate and perceptive insights and opportunities to reflect on what it means to truly live. It feels like I've taken the journey with her, and I'm wiser for it.

~Shay Youngblood,
author of *Soul Kiss* and *Black Girl in Paris*

Muhammad Ali, the boxer, activist and poet, once said, "If you see the world at forty the same way you saw the world at twenty, you've wasted twenty years of your life." This book is a living testimony to the fact that poet Sherry Quan Lee has been walking, crawling, swimming and dancing through the decades of her life wide awake, learning to face this world's many terrors without flinching – learning to find and savor its many small moments of grace where others may miss them, hiding in plain sight. As much as anything, *Septuagenarian* chronicles the poet's march, over a lifetime, toward self-knowledge, self-actualization and fearlessness. There are glimpses here of how, in her earlier years, it was an awkward dance...one step forward, two steps back. As a wiser, wilder, freer, white-haired krone, the march has become much more sure-footed and relentless. The book is a brave little chronicle of how life looks to her after seventy years on this earth. And no matter how many years you, yourself, have notched, you'll find it to be a welcome and worthy companion on your own journey.

~ David Lawrence Grant, screen-writer, nonfiction writer and teacher; author of essays in *Blues Vision: Writing from Black Americans* and *A Good Time for the Truth*

In *Septuagenarian*, Sherry Quan Lee connects the dots of her existence, including life before her life began. As she says, "every dot matters." She is an amalgam of all of the dots, including the loss of love, the father who was separated from his country and, eventually, separated from the family he made in America, including the mother who chose to separate from color, but who was still a descendent of enslaved Africans forced into the labor that powered American capitalism, including sexual violence, and the grief she "gently wraps in forgiveness." As we experience in all of Lee's work, we meet a fearless poet in these pages, precisely rendering associations that lead us to ultimate truths that are unexpected and fortuitous. As a Black and Chinese woman taught to pass for white as a child, racial identity and racial erasure have been looming themes. For a woman who turns seventy, other questions emerge. At the same time, she acknowledges the coalescence of maturation and blessings. Longing, hunger, and youthful desperation lessen. She entitles the fourth section of the book, *I Have No Regrets but Now*. Instead of regrets, what exists now is deep knowing. There are no masks to wear. There is exquisite specificity of a daring heart. Lee brings you close enough to hear it beat and tells you a profound story in verse that can save a life. As Sherry Quan Lee suggests, even if we cannot save the world, we can learn to save our own lives.

~ Sherrie Fernandez-Williams, author of *Soft: A Memoir*

Septuagenarian

LOVE IS WHAT HAPPENS WHEN I DIE

SHERRY QUAN LEE

Modern History Press

Ann Arbor, MI

ISBN 978-1-61599-568-4 paperback
ISBN 978-1-61599-569-1 hardcover
ISBN 978-1-61599-570-7 eBook

Published by
Modern History Press
5145 Pontiac Trail
Ann Arbor, MI 48105

Tollfree 888-761-6268   info@ModernHistoryPress.com
Fax 734-663-6861   www.ModernHistoryPress.com

Distributed by Ingram Group (USA/CAN/AU), Bertram's
Books (UK/EU)

What must I give more death to today,
in order to generate more life?
— Clarissa Pinkola Estés

Dedication

I Blame It on Education

Knowledge makes me more aware, it makes me more conscious. 'Knowing' is painful because after 'it' happens I can't stay in the same place and be comfortable. I am no longer the same person I was before. —Gloria Anzaldúa

My world on fire!

Kindling: *Maria Damon, Edén Torres, Linda Hogan, Nellie Wong, Nikki Giovanni, David Mura;*

Cave Canem & Asian American Renaissance.

I keep a heart full of poems burning.

Know where you've been, but don't live in the past. Know where you are going...but the most important thing is to know who you are.
—Shay Youngblood

Contents

Love Imagined

One doesn't have to imagine love, if one is love.

Exorcism

Baby born silent, silent as her mother's wound;
still waters. Not a wave. Not a storm.

Mother was not ripe or willing.

Parthenogenesis. Father worked nights.
Sister was ten months old(er).

    Silence. Invisibility. A small room to be born in.

Possessed, I held my breath, hoping death.

* * * * * *

My Chinese father was absent, invisible.
Did he see me in my mother's image and disappear?

Did he fear the afterbirth, smell the placenta?

Did he want my mother to stop loving him?

Did he want the baby girls not to be born?

Father ran through my veins like the money he spent gambling.
Was a blue-beaded bracelet what he had bet on; bet against

the girl baby, bet against me.

Mother never wore pink—or black.

* * * * * *

2

I rose to the occasion from my own need to be born.
I couldn't swim, but I didn't drown.

My mother rode the river well;
I cursed and stomped and sank.

Death frequent.

mouth closed, legs open

I rose to be pinched and prodded, pushed and pulled,
cradled and craved—devoured.

I rose to see snakes. Fear snakes. Eat snakes. Curse snakes.
Seek snakes. Rely on snakes. Snakes bigger than a fist. Snakes
smaller than a pinky finger.

And then I rose
        to hear a womyn's voice. I liked her tenor—
        charismatic as a Baptist priest. I was infused
        with pleasure; born again and again.

Daydreams and nightmares. Demons gone.

Night Tremors

A brown baby stretches
kicking white sheets

don't hold me
to your American history

the large print puzzle has
landed on the floor *nonsense*

someone says, *the questions*
and the answers are always the same

but, baby can't sleep
pulls blankie over her head

history lives in her bed.

The weight a child wears
bears so much room for sadness.

Every morning, a woman searches
for answers to a difficult puzzle
for a man who isn't there, a life
that isn't hers, a story that repeats;

sheets made of yesterday
that smell like sorrow, past
dream and nightmare.

Rite of Passage

*To imagine love is to believe love exists. To
imagine love is to see between the lies—the truth
that must be written.* —Sherry Quan Lee

I think amidst all this terror I am alone
as I journey through this shroud toward love.

I hustle past the blues towards
      jazz, a mixing of sky of bird
            of thunder of flight;
fear ebbs and flows

      hand to mouth
      safety always a concern.

         I can't see within the skin, the bones, the blood
         of my body—the fear of my own nature distant
         like the galaxy not yet reached.

Sometimes it frightens me, not knowing how I will die.
I'm not afraid of when;

         the world is a large body of terror where good
  and evil coexist,
      and each of us is responsible.

I can die if God wants me to, but not today;
today I am outside looking in and love is quiet.

Because She Is Old

...and if you think you will survive by hiding who
you really are, you are sadly misled...—June Jordan

She carries on each particle of memory in a bag;
bag lady, no one is looking.

Remember painting with only a brush and water and pictures
magically appeared? What portrait is she uncovering?
Does she have value? Is she beautiful now?

Does resurrection supersede death?

This passenger is going nowhere fast because the width
and the breadth of her world is inconsequential;
no safety checks are required. The risk of flying
too exhausting.

The characters in her journey too numerous for longevity,
too temporary for love.

Between blue air and white windows she surrenders.

I am that child uncovering the trajectory of who I am,
time is fleeting.

Remember the dot to dot coloring books? Every dot matters,
every connection from one number to another number matters.

What does surrender look like?

Once she was invisible because she was light-skinned
and she grew up passing for white.

Now she is invisible because she is old, a gray-haired specter amidst many gray-haired specters.

Invisibility a pro and a con.

She sees the bounty of the items in her bag flying out beyond constrictions. Angel wings.

afterword

The journey doesn't end on this page. I will turn another page, and another, forward and back.

Sometimes, we just need a break to breathe again,
a sprained ankle to know we really do want to write again.

It's enough to know numbers sometimes lie; it is enough
to know we can still make a difference.

Genealogy

*Trying to forgive and understand those of my
relatives who have chosen to pass for white has
been one of the most difficult ethical challenges of
my life...* —Adrian Piper

I will only appear
if you love me, my lineage

tainted by J. Crow, yet
cells inside our bodies

replicate and revise.
I do want it—family,

whoever you are, to come clean
and reveal yourselves—not

who you were or can be.

I am not yet a sibling,
(they told me otherwise)
not even a daughter
(mother wanted a white one)

we all, in my family pretend(ed)
we are somebody we're not.

What Preceded Today

I cannot be who you want me to be so you can love me.
You cannot love me because of who you are.
—Sherry Quan Lee

What preceded today was slavery—a plantation, a plantation
owner's son, my great-grandmother, my grandmother,
my mother, and me.

Grandpa and Grandma Franklin and Child

What preceded today was genocide.

The United States was the powerful, the uncolored.

What preceded today were decades of no rights, uncivil rights,
peaceful and not so peaceful protests for rights.

What preceded today was a family, my family, battered—
before it even became a family.

I was not womyn, merely *commodity.*

What preceded today was and is capitalism. On the backs
of African/Americans with whom I share DNA.

On the backs of all people forced into labor.

On the backs of those with no rights.

On the backs of those who didn't even have the right
to have the backs of their loved ones.

Backs that were separated—enslaved; backs that were slashed,
hung; backs that were murdered—Black backs.

You know you don't love the me that is defiant, that is angry,
that needs to know what preceded me, that needs to know
what separates me, that separates us, that needs to understand

why my family—my siblings, why I can't do unconditional.

I hold my grief gently, wrap it in forgiveness, add it to a list
of sorrows that preceded me.

A History of Separation

If you are free, you are not predictable, and you are
not controllable. —June Jordan

Is it love when death never happens because
love is preceded by separation, by segregation?

She sees her head separated from her body; her body
says yes, her head says not now. Yet, over and over
again she is chattel.

History says her white lover can have her,
but can't marry her. But they tie a knot anyway.

It unravels. The first marriage, the second, the third,
and the fourth.

History says she is nothing, but someone else's
property; too often she's equated *property* with love.

There were professors and ministers and other
low-down no-good men who

she thought had good intentions, but separation
from them was necessary.

Only the blues seemed permanent.

At seventy madness is a pleasure and a respite.
I was never insane.

I flourish in texture and color and pattern. I am not
in the center, but gravity doesn't hold me down.

I endeavor not to control, but be out of control, but mostly
not to be controlled.

    The woman I loved, a footnote.

Separation Preceded Me

My father immigrated to California from Canton, China.
He was eleven
> separated from his country
> separated from his family

>   he worked selling vegetables to send money
>   *home* to his widowed mother.

My mother was born in Minnesota; her mother, daughter
of a slave mistress, migrated from Georgia, married Grandpa,
a pullman porter, who also escaped the South, separated
from *home* and family.

Mother chose, before or after she married my dad,
to pass for white;

Mother chose passing as passage toward safety
for herself/and her children;

she chose to separate from a color line that preceded her
(but, mama, you are still Black).

Father chose to leave my mother, when I was five, for another
white woman and more mixed-race children;

Mother chose celibacy until the day she died;

at nineteen, I chose to leave my mother.

Father never returned to China; Mother never returned
to being Black;

and here I am knowing—that love guarantees separation.

A History of Sexual Relations

I want them to remember. Me too.

China Doll

I am not a China doll. I am not Oriental.
Exotic. Fantasy.

I'm not.

I wear my mandarin collar,
my frog closures

for me.

Because I can. Because I am.

I wear my silk. My brocade.

I am beautiful.

Aggressive. Powerful. Independent.

Okay, some stereotypes were me.
      Silent.
      Passive.
      Accommodating.

      Were me.

History Won't Win

Mama said,
    cover yourself with lies
        but deceit couldn't outwit me

painted with powder and gloss, my portrait was
promiscuous

    I meant not to look back
    at men
        men who loved who they thought I was
        men who loved who they wanted me to be;

after their arrogance, after each evening of bloodletting
I battled with *knowing crazy* believing I was nothing
except giving.

I was seductress, while all the time posing; lying was effortless

    what was then more complicit is now more critique.

I have words for and against all madness; madness: the fact
that I wasn't who I am.

Madness is a mother not wanting to protect yet another child,
wanting the child to be a different child, another white child.

Madness is another child without knowledge, without lessons,
without instructions—without history, without language.

Fear came from what I didn't know. I was taught to be afraid.
But I didn't know what I was afraid of.

Guns in White Rooms

There are guns in white rooms, loaded;
men with ammunition.

There he is, there he is
in a room larger
than his small experience,

loving a proud brown woman.

She dares him to put down his gun,
however, the love of an uncocked
man
        she has yet to know.

Haunted House

There is a ghost hovering over my bed,
next to my writing table.

I dislike his presence, his intrusion;
each memory a warning.

I light candles, sprinkle holy water,
burn sage

     I keep my heart crossed, my poems flowing.

There is something about the ghost of a man
that is familiar, ancestral

that clings to me like my great-*white*-grandfather.

Memoir

I'm tired of confessional poetry
the clenched teeth, the sadness;
opening the heart to expose
the vulnerability that both saves
and destroys a woman.

I recognized a man on tv news
wondered if he'd recognize me,
how I needed him, forty-five years
ago, to save me.

A married man of the cloth, to him
I confessed *I am crazy.*

In the basement, of a faulty church,
God's disciple took advantage
of a young woman seeking prayer,
seeking refuge;

instead, she received an unholy ghost

> *a slave in the white house bedroom*
> *a noose around her neck.*

This task, of trying to rewrite the story,
doesn't go away, it doesn't get easier;
it circles like a crow patiently awaiting
the carnage.

A History of Rape

But if we would speak the unspeakable, if we
would name and say the source of our sorrow and
scars...we should show to the world, at last, that
shame belongs with blame, not on the victim.
— June Jordan

What if I had named my rapist(s)?

What if I had named my rapist(s) and reminded them
when they raped me?

What if I had named my rapist(s) and reminded them
where they raped me?

What if I had named my rapist(s) and reminded them
how they raped me?

What if *me too* exposed *he too* and I named him and
I named him and I named

each *he too* on my list of *me too?* Memory jolted.

Re-remembered—

remembered........

I almost died. Suicide. I want *them* to remember. *Me too.*

I'm Not Letting Go of Desire

it's not the enemy.

Oh, there were men, there was a woman, there were moments;
there was the body lying to the heart, there was the heart
lying to the body.

No regrets, I was searching for an answer to my needs.

Rape is another story

me too is not new, not unspoken—our stories archived

we have been raped, and raped, and gang raped

someone put a gun to my head

what if we had been loved?

It's Always About the Mother

shut doors and closed windows

Mother's and Mine

1.
Mother lived to be eighty-six years old. I'll be damned
if every lifetime bruise didn't show itself on her predeath
body. They were big bruises. And grew larger as I watched
her die. I didn't bother to count them. I've been counting
them every day since I was born. They were black
and they were blue.

2.
I no longer search for the answers.
Asking the questions is enough.

3.
After death do bruises disappear? The doctor said Mom
had a leukemia blast. This, after he and we all agreed
leukemia wasn't what was killing her. It was her heart.
Black (and blue).

*Mother, white is not a color. Your sisters dealt with Black
in other ways—marrying it, cursing it, celebrating it.*

4.
Mother went to a one-room high rise. Went to her room
and locked the door. Sometimes I knocked. Once-in-awhile
she answered. Responding most favorably to candy kisses,
romance novels, and lottery tickets. Where is it I want to go?

5.
Bruises are painful, colorful reminders that one has been hit.
Or has walked into foreign objects. I run away again and again.
Open the first door I see and slam into dysfunction. *Mother,
is it you I keep running into?*

6.
Mother, what is it I haven't yet recognized? What gifts did you
try to give me? If, from wherever you are now, you could make
my bruises go away, would you?

7.
Mother wanted me married. She wanted the white lieutenant
to sing his way out of *South Pacific* and marry all three
of her Chinese daughters. Did she know I might prefer Liat?

Why, Mother,

did you want for your daughters that which you refused
for yourself? What was it about my father?
Bloody Mary chewed betel nuts. Where was her husband?

8.
My friend says she's a trauma drama queen. I said,
you're not. I thought, *is that what I am, a trauma*
drama queen? Sounds flamboyant. Sounds self-serving.
Sounds tiring. How many times have I run away?

9.
Happiness is an emotion. A damn good one. I've decided
to be happy.

10.
How can I explain this happiness, this wealth of bruises?
My hands hurt. My legs are stiff. I have a headache.

11.
And still, another bruise won't let me sleep. I can't see it.
I can't name it. Did I forget to say, *I'm sorry?* If I didn't
say, *I'm sorry,* is it too late? *Mom, I miss you.*

12.
I was afraid the things you told me when I was a child

were true. The bag of bones in the basement and
the butter man. The shoemaker. The high school boy.
But, why, Mother, were you afraid of the women?
Your sisters, the neighbor ladies, and your daughters?

13.
Sometimes I feel like a boxer punching myself. I reverberate.
The good thing is, some things shake loose. *Mom, I'm sorry*
I ran away.

14.
Maybe I should go to the basement and throw away more
of who I am not.

15.
A big bruise is centered in my belly. The world is heavy.
Like stale gum chewed and forgotten. A wad in the mouth
in the morning.

I am fifty-two years old and breathing heavy. Is there anything
wrong with desire? When I lie down in bed, I drool.
A slobbering idiot I've become. Sometimes, I just wake up sad.

16.
I know when the bruise is dormant. It watches. It listens.
I know. But I forget.

17.
I always loved my mother.

18.
Perhaps I am happy because death is just a sunrise or two away
and it must be beautiful. Or perhaps I am happy because
I am not dead. Anxiety, where are you? Oh well, goodbye.

19.
When I stopped wanting what I couldn't have, I bruised

less often. When I stopped beating myself up because
ugly and stupid were words I made up, my vocabulary
grew and I bruised less often. When I stopped lashing out,
I bruised less often. When I stopped acquiescing, I bruised
less often. When I stopped all the lies, I bruised less often.

When I realized how much I loved womyn, men
were suddenly human and I bruised less often.

20.
I pay attention to my bruises, turn them into stories
and watch them disappear.

21.
A bruise is temporary. The dent in the car. The pinch
in the butt. The blank page. A bruise appears. Disappears.
No stitches. No scars. No attachments. No prolonged
anger. No hate.

22.
There are flowers everywhere and birds. Bamboo plants
and tiger lilies. A cardinal this morning. My garden
is a small room. Bruises are beautiful. They are not harmful.
They are not slit wrists, a drug overdose, or a hung rope.
I have given up poison. Cigarettes. Bologna. Self-doubt.

My prayers are no longer petitions, but praise. Tomorrow
I might stumble. The bruise will be beautiful. Love is so easy.

23.
Bruises are like lilacs. Beautiful in bloom, and seasonal.

24.
Mother hit me. I was prepubescent, a crying girl. The yardstick
broke into splinters of heartache. Mother's and mine. It was all
about love.

Mother couldn't say she wanted it. She couldn't risk
her daughter wanting it. She had many yardsticks.

Is death opportunity or loss?

25.
Father wanted to be Western. Wanted America. Although
his trip on the U.S.S. China wasn't his choice,
he made it his reality.

Where is my father's boat now? I want to get on it. I want
to return to a place neither of us knows. But I won't leave
in chaos. I won't leave crying or screaming. I won't leave
not knowing where I'm going.

26.
The answer is in the words of my dying mother: *Get out
of my hospital room. I want to be alone.*

27.
The answer is in the words of my response: *I love you.
I am not leaving. I know who I am.*

28.
My bruises are the love I keep running away from.

Silence

Mother's words were sewn shut, stitched
like the four identical dresses worn by my sisters
and me, hand crafted by Mother's intuition;
likeness creates invisibility.

We looked like all the neighborhood girls,
although our hair was black our legs thin,
our feet small.

I even went to the Lutheran Church, and prayed
to God the Father almighty because my Chinese father
disappeared. I never knew *Chinese*, although
I tried by playing mahjong on hot summer days
and teaching the neighborhood girls

(it gets complicated who was fitting into whose life)

and chicken sub gum chow mein was just part
of my diet like Campbell's Soup and Wonder Bread
and turkeys from the Salvation Army at Christmas.
At Christmas our dresses were red velvet and frilly
and girly until they weren't;

and they were simple and seductive—maybe
that's when the silence was broken. Not with words,
but with images and faith that stitches could be
undone; but it would take work—the skill of a crafts-
woman: an artist, a magician, a hair stylist because

one of us had thick curly hair like Mother's, one of us
had silky straight hair like Father's; and, yes, one was
beauty and one shame/hot combs and gas flames and
it was complicated pretending

to be someone else in order to escape being who we were.

I wonder if Mother desired the language and permission
to say what it is like to be a Black woman passing
for white and her right

to be safe; but neighbors had guns. Mother shut doors
and closed windows, locked in four daughters,
(but not the son).

Father was on the run with his mistress. Father wanted
to be white like my mother wanted to be white,

but neither of them

spoke to the other of desire each reaching for the gold
pot differently. One by hiding (mother), one by buying

things: a washer a dryer a mangle a steam bath a television
an outdoor fireplace a flagstone patio and cigars (father).

The children sat on red stairs to their blue bedroom, didn't
know what to make of the bickering; but they felt safe.
How could they fear what they didn't know? They ate
the raspberry Jell-O with bananas and grapes hiding

the relatives helped too because in our neighborhood
Blacks were banned from entering the Church until
the new minister and his wife arrived with three
adopted Black children. But, even then I had to be

cautious

and wore white to communion as if white could
forgive my sins. Still the minister walked by me
with the wafers and the wine as if he didn't know

32

I was a member of the congregation, a voice
in the choir. Maybe wearing white was uppity of me,

although

I had been wearing white since the day I was born;
so, I looked for other gods in other neighborhoods.

Eventually,

I understood why mother withheld her words,
and her desire.

Children get lost in the silences. Love has to be
large, larger than a mother's secrets.

It's Always About the Mother

Stepped on a crack broke my mother's back

each deliberate step a breath to count, a heartbeat;

but there is no concrete sidewalk to guide me, only
cracks to break—the rhythm of forgetfulness, and
observation.

My memory is prisoner to my mother's deception;
my sons are prisoner to my candor.

It's always about the mother.

Mother went out of her way to deceive me. So far out

of her way she *stepped on a crack and broke
her mother's back*—this I don't know to be true.

Did my grandmother admonish my mother for turning
her back on being Black? Or, did she applaud her?

I know I *stepped on my mother's back* by un-passing;
and, my children *stepped on my back* by paying me no mind—
      I don't know if this is true.

I can't live my mother's life; my children can't live mine.

My mother died when she was eighty-six, she was

almost ready *she was waiting for the world to end*;

I am seventy and heavy into contemplation.

The Curse of Color

*We are never free from the feeling that we have
failed. We are never free from self-loathing. We are
never free from the feeling that something is wrong
with us, not with the world that made this mess.'*
       —Jesmyn Ward

If I could have imagined my brown babies suffering
would I have said, no?

Would I have pushed back, kept my legs crossed,
the cross of motherhood not salvation?

   * * *

I couldn't bring my babies forward
as I dreamt them—beyond poverty, beyond race;

  I'm not going to apologize.

   * * *

I can't stop them from trudging in muck stuck
in my fate, my phantom scars spread
like sadness, like grief.

  Everyone (white) seems
  so happy, so accomplished,
  so very, very good.

   * * *

I am seeing with a mad eye, perplexed.
Mothers can give what they can give:
I tried to give more.

  Is it anger I feel when

I compare your wealth to mine?

* * *

Have I cursed my sons
with the truth? I am not white.

Mother warned me.

I Didn't Know Men

I lived in a household of women. Men in my life
appeared when I disappeared.

What I discovered about men didn't teach me
to raise sons. I was still trying to rise above myself.

The white fathers were not helpful; arrogance
is what they brought to the dining room table
(and the bedroom); criticism is what they provided.

I loved my sons so much I abandoned them,
left them with their white father who could afford
to keep them.

I could run or I could stay. A lose lose situation.

I was not the mama I thought I could be. I was
not the love my sons understood.

Separation had a hold on who I was. I was
an accomplice to its power.

                    I forgive me.

I Have No Regrets, But Now

the onset of loss, a blessing and a curse

On the Eve of Her Seventieth Year

She lost the cigarettes, the scotch, the tension, the need
for attention. The routine of another day/breaking

brown girl

the urge not so urgent, but the need it doesn't disappear.
Goes quiet. Goes deep, seeps into isolation

the father the mother the siblings disappear.

Give her an opportunity, she says no; if she gives you a maybe,
it is still a no; even a yes is unreliable, but who's keeping score?

Who counts transitory friends and lovers?
An abacus isn't quick enough; but, the eye blinks
and, where were we?

She wants the drama back, if only to crack the safe
of loneliness and economy.

I have no regrets, but now...

the onset of loss, a blessing and a curse.

I Didn't Need to Save the World

Now that I am old(er)

the father, the mother, the siblings, the husband(s),
are missing. Gone.

Obsessions, gone.

*I am story. Nothing more than an unfinished story with a plot,
a theme, a who done it, and maybe even a why.*

*I am a newspaper headline; I will write my own obituary
because no one ever knew who I was.*

There is no epiphany

> *only day-to-day survival. And that is enough.*
> *I didn't need to save the world; only myself.*

Longing disappeared in the chaos, the living; hunger
no longer a snake wrapped around my leg.

I have lost so many people over time, but at seventy
long-term memory brings them back,

both the wicked and the wise. It's a caravan.

> *Oh so wild and oh so beautiful.*

Whatever road I would have taken would have ended
at the same destination.

Because it's story. And story ends where it begins.

I Woke to This Place

where anger has been replaced with forgiveness;
this place where I am healthy, where

I don't regret living. My children and grandchildren
are beautiful.

In this place, I am neither arrogant nor compliant;
courage and bravado came from a well now gone dry.

I now know there is a difference between opinion
and truth.

It's my heart

here, in this place, it's my heart that I relentlessly rattle
each beat marks my revival.

I don't regret my journey that has led me closer to death.

Every step of the way has been meaningful.

I was once pompous and unbearable. I believed everything
I heard or read that seemed to give me an answer to who I was;

my heart knew otherwise.

Perseverance got me to the place of where I am now

       where being alone isn't about loneliness, but a place
       where there is too much time.

I have too much time. Every day gets longer and longer,
each week, each month like a lengthy breath of sorrow,
       like a lifetime empty of love.

Suddenly, My Life Is Private

a space where dying is more on my mind than possibility

> *death, I welcome you*
> *(dying, I am afraid)*

Grandma is different than mother. Retirement is different than career.

Vision changes. And location. And technology.

And the body. One day I woke up and didn't recognize the flesh, the features, the downward slope.

Friends become keystrokes and FB photos.

Fractured. There is no one friend that fits me, no one community

don't blame it on age; separation has always been required.

I float between communities that don't interact

> *social, cultural, political—literary*

enough to make wise use of my time, days lingering.

Most days I don't travel farther than the internet; most days the *net* is enough.

I Have Yet to Learn How to Pray

The thing about God is sometimes they are vague.

Mother prayed every night for eighty-five years,
for everyone she loved—

Dear God, keep my children and my grandchildren safe.

Except, one night she forgot to say her prayers.
       And something terrible happened.
              And she thought it was her fault.

I don't know how to pray.

Like a kid at Christmas I ask for gifts—
       random requests when I want something:
       wellbeing, safe travel, world peace—love.

It's selfish, I know.

Even when I praise God, I expect their respect.

God forgive my foolish petitions.

God forgive my lack of faith.

I Have No Regrets, but Now

love; one day, if that's all I'm given, it's enough.
I have always loved much too much, but such
is not necessary or reliable.

Where in the World

you love in mine

How to Live

with someone else's privilege,
to love   in an atmosphere

of passivity

where freedom is clearly not
in her favor; *where in the world*

caution and suspicion are heavily
relied on; where trust is an issue

of equality, unless she lies. Black

is not a solid color and yellow
belongs to a car named Buttercup.

White is transparent, not ever
never a color; yet, he's chosen
his rainbow and named her love

where in the world in his world
rainbows are pretty, and even smart.

His friends will be happy for him—

and not even notice, at first, that she's
complicated and not white.

He remains welded in his world,
where in the world

she is breaking/her heart

knowing he can never
live in hers.

It Sounds Like an Excuse to Me

I'm not sure   why we have to be so justified,
what we need is justice.

I deplore the bullet in my chest, the knife in my back
we are divisive and our lives are at risk.

I won't go so far as to whine *where is the diversity*
in my private life; I won't admit it's my fault.

But, I'm not a bridge. I never said I was. I never chose
to be living in a white world one moment, a world of color
the next, unable to shuffle the two together.

It's not a choice; it is, perhaps, Minnesota, where,
ironically, mixed relations are abundant.

Whatever it is, it is no longer my lie, my mask.
Nikki Giovanni once told me not to be so hard on myself.

I hope it's not too late to consider the world.

Language Is a Difficult Way to Communicate

Words are difficult for me. But I have story.

My family had no words. Only secrets. We ate and we drank, and we said nothing.

I have pictures in my mind of what was, but no words.

I see my mother at the kitchen table with our neighbor lady.

They are drinking Hills Brothers coffee, smoking Pall Mall cigarettes, and eating gingersnap cookies.

What do they have in common? Mother, the passing for white single parent of five kids; the white neighbor lady, married, mother of one.

I clutch coffee, alone. Pretend to have a conversation.
Drink up excuses, avoid the truth.

The truth is my world is larger than a red Formica table.
Larger than black or white.

But, how to write larger than an image or a dream?

I have what my mother didn't, a college education,
but I don't know what she knew.

The Difference Between Opinion and Authority

Oh, how I love the mundane. Wildflowers and calico kittens.

Sometimes we don't get what we want. We expect friends

to *show* what we want to hear;

       we want to believe in each other.

I'm also guilty of *telling*, as if I'm an authority.

Tolerate is a word I don't want in my vocabulary.
I find it difficult to remain calm;

      why do I let your opinions provoke me,
      as if my opinions trump yours?

An apocalypse of language makes communication impossible

Can poetry save us?

Where in the World

is history forgotten? There are signs everywhere:
confederate flags and statues, swastikas, and rope—
there are graves.

1948, the year I was born, the United Nations declared
genocide a crime; however, *ethnic cleansing* was okay.[1]

Where is the humanity?

The year is 2020, white men with assault rifles have
their temperatures checked; black men and black women
are riddled with tear gas and (rubber) bullets.

Racism is a public health crisis.

The year is 2020. I am seventy-two. A white man wearing
a white hood is simply asked to leave; a black man wearing
a hoodie...

There is no justice.

Where in the world does a pandemic unify?
Where in the world does a president make sure that it divides?

We are here, the children of the vanished; we are here
burning, yearning to survive.

---

[1] https://www.history.com/topics/holocaust/ethnic-cleansing

But the Truth Is

Love is not a *whimper*. I love me to death takes *bang*.

Who knows love beyond paved roads where death
is temporary, a haven of dis/comfort?

I don't belong here cloistered/wrapped in a white world
where words don't have bang;

       but history, my history, implodes on a regular
       irregular heartbeat.

I have yet to walk the road in the woods alone
afraid to run into danger—afraid to live,
afraid to love;

afraid to admit, I want the world *where in the world
you love in mine.*

Mirror Mirror

*You can look in the mirror every day and never really
see yourself.*—Wing Young Huie

I look in the mirror more often, not less.
I want to know who I see.

*Yesterday, she wondered who she looked like
perception skewed by who she was supposed to be—
white girl.*

I want to know who you see.

*She wondered what you thought she looked like
because notions of herself were unreliable.*

I am not frantic, or desperate, or afraid—
I'm bi-curious.

*Do you see the African American womyn
hidden in her mother's lies?*

*Do you see her Chinese father who disappeared
when she was five?*

The charade is over. I didn't create it; it created me.

This Year Love

It's about death. Each death a rebirth.

It's About Love

You will love again the stranger who was your self.
—Derek Walcott

Love is looking in a mirror and seeing grace.

Love is looking in a mirror and seeing dignity.

Love is looking in a mirror and seeing humility.

Love is looking in a mirror and seeing forgiveness.

* * *

Love, no longer a terror, a torment, a grief, an insecurity—a lie.

Love, not a Minnesota winter or Seattle rain. *It's about death.*

I love me to death, the Black Chinese (white) Womyn I was.

The Boy and the Girl, the Man and the Woman

He is the man who remembers the boy and remembers the girl.
I am the woman who remembers the girl who was in love
with the boy.

He was the boy who moved forward; I was the girl who
stepped back. *Remembering, I am Black.*

He is the man who was the boy battered by clergy;
I am the woman who was the girl sleeping with clergy.

He is the man who was the boy who married the woman
who undressed in the closet while he loved the girl who didn't.

I am the woman who was the girl who chose not to live
in anyone's closet.

I was the girl who grew into the womyn who grew into words,
into voice—into visibility, and self-love.

The Conversation

Just say thank you. And she did.
Emptied pockets of *no regrets.*
Removed risk and shame, and
a few pretensions.

Love, a trickster.

Who is, who is unassuming?
Who is, who never falls apart?

(He whose heart has never been
broken.)

Who are you she says, *dare I love you?*

Who Are You?

You who say I am beautiful
and kiss each spot of age you find
on this wrinkled map of a body

who are you that you trust
I will love you, despite
roads of mistrust
that have led nowhere safe?

Who are you that lives
at the edge of nowhere
a town unlike a city,
a one-way life with few
distractions?

Say, again,

I love you, say you have read my life.

I read your heart scars like a sorcerer
reads palms; my wounds healing.

Who are we that the world exists
without us, that we exist in a whirl
of exclusivity

>   eating the green, the fresh, the spice,
>   the juice, the body, the heart.

Our lips gateway to tongues speaking
in a language we are just now learning.

Age Has Everything to Do With It

Permission to write this poem, to weave this story.
To hold the hand to touch the narrative.

Not all relationships are volatile. Not this one.
Age has everything to do with it.

They meet for the first time in a park and it's raining.

She places a cross on the picnic bench, unsure
if it's necessary. Not knowing she is protected
by organic food and lack of devilish intent.

If needed, there is an umbrella; but truth weathers
gray skies and intuition.

They break bread and sip jasmine tea. *This is love,*
or so she reckoned, not just another walk in the woods.

Septuagenarian

and if ever i touched a life i hope that life knows /
that I know that touching was and still is and will
always / be the true / revolution —Nikki Giovanni

Seven is always someone's lucky number;
ten times seven years baby boomers
age like fine wine. I've matured.

Born choking on air thick with hope,
this rat survives, thrives in ways
I'm not supposed to.

This civil rights advocate didn't know in the sixties that
she didn't have rights, neither did she know that she did.

Passing for white not knowing I wasn't,
complicated perspective.

Was not knowing *I am beautiful* a fear
of pride, or an admittance of shame?

She knows, even if she had loved herself,
her journey would not have been
charming because there will always be
those who won't love a mixed-race girl.

Years of an inadequate education were
marked by white men hypocrites and liars
(who surely were miffed by my impertinence).

She lost friends and family and lovers over the year;
although wearisome, it was necessary.
She knew the revolution is not everyone's cup of tea.

In my seventieth year my reflection is daunting.
I didn't save the world nor was I trying to.
But on my way toward love, I saved me.

You may have benefited from her recovery
or found her despicable when she stepped
on your privilege; either way her impact
has been noted.

Forgiveness is supposed to be salvation and
I forgive, but forgetting may be more useful.

To be love, to love, to be loved is pure joy!
Even if it takes seventy years to be noted.

Oh, Holy God

let the *difficult* seep deep
into seeds of relief

let the *difficult* abandon
all grieving

> *they had their reasons*
> *you had yours*

I can die today, and I did; love was easy,
a narrow passage, a river crossed

no more loves lost

angel riffs

hallelujah cliffs,

> the garden tilled; love, a fallow myth.

Oh, Holy God!

A wake where flowers grow where ashes rest.

Pandemic

and then death was real

Apocalypse Twenty-First Century

Millennials write about the apocalypse;
they dance in the streets dressed as zombies.

Not just a yearly ritual, they are daily consumed
in science fiction; they write and perform their
well-crafted plays—and then

death was real.

A pandemic arrived to confirm their suspicions;
sheltered in isolation, they kept writing.

Others, trumpers and trumpettes took to the beaches;
pointing their swords toward the elderly;

everyone needs a scapegoat—

grandmas and grandpas beware!

Love Is What Happens

*When I dare to be powerful... it is less and less
important if I am afraid.* —Audre Lorde

one breath at a time; a fever, the chills.

The world needs me now; the world
needs my voice.

I hear *fearful* I see me brave.

We know who will die next. Are we ready
to end the pandemic

of hate your neighbor, hate the person
that isn't you?

I am ready to survive

pomp and circumstance. Where was I

when the lights went out, the hospitals
overflowed, the elderly dead?

We were together, love, but I was afraid.

There is a man on a pedestal, but he's not you.
Pedestals collapse;

the brave write far into the night

one courageous word at a time; one compelling
book at a time

(we survived our literary differences, or we didn't).

We were seventy and the world didn't end;
but we were never the same.

Isolation was the norm; I reveled in it.

unburdened, unashamed

I made my bed daily.

Obituary

She had died once / and once was enough /
to know she could die /

And that would be that, / but she could not return /
and live without stars.—Ana Castillo

I woke to a lengthy obituary, a sermon
really. It was carved in a dream.

I transcribed what was vividly remembered
as I sipped my morning coffee, as I tasted

your muffin of oats and flax, pumpkin seeds
and walnuts.

You were in your usual comfort zone
on the couch with your computer

searching, didn't matter the question
the answer was always your heart.

I could reach across the dining room table
to the couch, and touch us—our thoughts
coincide.

Our obituary is lovely. *The couple*
died of all things preceding them,
except stars.

Stars held them through the night
of the election, the year of the pandemic;

their hearts still beating beyond death.

Oh! This is the dream, a metaphor
of too many words.

Love happened.

The world didn't die.

Morning Glories

*There are days we live / as if death were nowhere /
in the background...*—Li-Young Lee

But, not today. Today death is flourishing. And it is love,
but not lovely.

It is love, but it is lonely. It is grief, and it is hardening.
Death, today,

is what you expect of love. The complications. The heart
serrated like a ripe tomato and the juice bleeds

across corn fields and apple orchards.

When he shouts (I don't know who he is, he could be anyone)

they are everywhere, blocks and blocks of Black people. I hate

them. I hate them. I hate Black people

echoes across blue sky, and white clouds. *I hate them* drifts
like gunshots

south of the city where more than deer or wild turkeys
are at risk.

I hate them

doesn't sound like fear, but worse—disgust. South of the city
where there are not *blocks of them*. Where even in the summer

it is cold; it is winter white.

71

I could live without death, but I can't love without it. I am the Black womyn you can't see, but I can hear you.

I am standing on the weathered deck next door.

Hate travels.

Separation is a safety device, a lock on my door, not yours. Where do *Black Lives Matter* along these secluded roads?

Today I've escaped,

if only momentarily, to write this poem and retrieve my breath.

Morning glories, like love, take months to bloom, but only live one day at a time.

And When I Die

Love is larger than life, a world
gone mad, a world dying.

A world where chance is a marathon
those who run with it, those who
retreat.

I run the risk
of loving
(another man who is white).

Heartbeats belong to the dead
and the babies; love seeps
from one dead generation
to the living.

My children are okay, no more
demons. Boys to men they
know love, are loved, like
mothers they love their children.
I no longer grieve, I breathe
my loves.

We surge together what is broken
for another glimpse of love.
Perhaps, the heart
broken is what saves us;

perhaps, if we love for only one day
it's enough.

When love happens, it will be
the death of me.

I've always said so.

The world and the poets know
this to be true.

Found Poem

that's when the silence is broken

The World Is Heavy

One doesn't have to imagine good and evil amidst
all this terror.

Sadness, the bones and the blood surrender

  but, we can make a difference we are all somebody

  we are not on the backs on the backs on the backs
  of sorrow

  that preceded

  head separated from body
  body separated from country
  family separated

love guarantees memory
  guns in white rooms the ghost
  of a man an unholy ghost trying to rewrite the story

what if what if what if asking the questions is [not] enough?

    sometimes madness

I feel like a boxer punching the world
is heavy that's when the silence is broken
not with words but with images children

didn't know what to make of the bickering
children got lost in the silence suffering;

the father the mother the siblings gone
a newspaper headline.

To the wicked and the wise *there is a difference*
between opinion and truth, a space where
freedom Is clearly not where in the world we are

divisive and our lives are at risk.

Tolerate is a difficult word. Racism, white men
with assault rifles. Death

is temporary.

History implodes on a regular irregular heartbeat

like a sorcerer reads palms this is love choking on air
ready to survive   pedestals
        collapse amidst a pandemic

as I sip my morning coffee the heart/broken
is what saves us. The charade is over

this year. Hallelujah! Hallelujah! Hallelujah!

Writing Exercise

January 6, 2021, insurrection at the Capitol, death—lies. A culmination of four frightful years. How, as a poet, can we respond? We could use the fast and flowing media coverage to write a found poem rearranging and reformatting what has already been written by journalists, by reporters, by politicians. Or, we can turn to our own writing.

Using only text from *Septuagenarian: love is what happens when I die,* I randomly chose words and phrases and strung them together. What might be hidden if we break apart the whole? Have I, unknowingly, moved beyond the personal— *have I entered the world?*

I discovered within my memoir of verse that I was saying more than I had said, that for me the personal continues to be political, and all things are temporary. The memory of what has preceded me implodes and love is my act of survival.

Use words and phrases from what you have previously written and *find* a poem. Perhaps you will discover what you didn't know you knew. It may not, at first, make sense, yet it will.

Afterword

A Crown of No Regret

I have a drive to break the secrets, because I think that
what we don't tell others, we often lie to ourselves
about. I am determined not to lie to myself.

—Toi Derricotte

Love Imagined: a mixed-race memoir took me *inward*, making
sense of my past-the Black/Chinese/Girl passing for white-,
exploring why I was who I was and why who I was couldn't
love or be loved—*why I wasn't love.*

Septuagenarian: love is what happens when I die, is my
outward swan song.

What may previously have been self-indulgent, confessional
writing, it was. I have no regrets. No shame.

However, the younger I was the less time I had the more
I accomplished. The older I am now, the more time I have;
have I accomplished anything? The critics ignore me.

My words were a road that led me, not out of the woods,
but into it. Out of tightly controlled spaces with no room
to breathe, and into a forest of freedom; not a sanctuary,
but an experience of nature that situates me into a cosmos
larger than myself, into a world where gratitude and
forgiveness are my daily bread, and fear's stronghold
is weakening, as it takes a backseat to love.

Acknowledgements

With gratitude to fellow septuagenarian, Peter Martin, who has shown me the possibility of love *after love imagined.*

To my readers, and editors, thank you for your generosity of time and critique: Anya Achtenberg, 신 선 영 辛善英 Sun Yung Shin, Deborah Keenan, Shay Youngblood, David Mura, Terri Taylor, Jay Sandvik, Lola Osunkoya, Pat Ronken, David Lawrence Grant, Sherrie Fernandez-Williams, Sandra Newbauer, Chris Stark, and Carolyn Holbrook.

Immense gratitude to Shirlee M. Scott for sharing her ideas about how the separation of Black families, since the buying and selling of slaves in America until present day incarceration of/and killing of Black men and women, could explain the separations within our/my family.

Much love to Edén Torres who knows my intention. She explains my poems to me beyond my emotional scope of them.

As always, a heartfelt appreciation goes out to my publisher, Victor Volkman, LI IP, Modern History Press, for believing I have something to say that needs to be said whether or not anyone is listening.

About the Author

Sherry Quan Lee, MFA, University of Minnesota, is the author of *Chinese Blackbird*, a memoir in verse; *How to Write a Suicide Note, serial essays that saved a woman's life*; *Love Imagined: a mixed-race memoir (*a Minnesota Book Award Finalist)*; and, the picture book *And You Can Love* Me *a story for everyone who loves someone with ASD*—all published by LHP, Modern History Press, Ann Arbor, MI. She is the editor of *How Dare We! Write: a multicultural creative writing discourse,* an anthology finding home in university writing classrooms.

Author's Previously Published Poems

"Where in the World," accepted for online publication in *A Moment of Silence*, July 2020.

"But the Truth Is," accepted for online publication in *A Moment of Silence*, July 2020.

"The Curse of Color," published in *Rocked by the Waters*, Nodin Press, eds. Hasse & Kildegaard, April 2020.

"Silence," *Haute Dish*, summer 2015, The Arts and Literature Magazine of Metropolitan State University, Volume 11, Issue 2.

* * *

"China Doll," *Chinese Blackbird*, Modern History Press, 2008, originally published by Asian American Renaissance, 2002.

"Mother's and Mine," *Chinese Blackbird*, Modern History Press, 2008, originally published by Asian American Renaissance, 2002.

"It's About Love," *How to Write a Suicide Note: serial essays that saved a woman's life*, Modern History Press, 2008.

"Exorcism," *How to Write a Suicide Note: serial essays that saved a woman's life*, Modern History Press, 2008.

Citations

Finalist - 27th annual Minnesota Book Awards (Memoir & Creative Nonfiction)

Critical Acclaim for Sherry Quan Lee's *Love Imagined*

"Joining the long history of women of color fighting to claim literary space to tell our stories, Sherry Quan Lee shares her truth with fierce courage and strength in *Love Imagined*. ... Quan Lee crafts a riveting tale of Minnesota life set within the backdrop of racial segregation, the Cold War, the sexual revolution while navigating it all through the lens of her multi-layered identities. A true demonstration of the power of an intersectional perspective."

> --Kandace Creel Falcón, Ph.D., Director of Women's and Gender Studies, Minnesota State University, Moorhead

"*Love Imagined*: this fascinating, delightful, important book. This imagining love, this longing for love. This poverty of No Love, this persistent racism, sexism, classism, ageism. The pain these evils cause the soul...This is an important document of a mixed-race contemporary woman, a memoir about her family lineages back to slavery, back to China, back to early Minneapolis, and about the struggle of finding herself in all of these."

> —Sharon Doubiago, author of *My Father's Love*

"When I read Sherry's story [*Love Imagined*], I recognized feelings and meanings that mirrored mine. I felt a sense of release, an exhale, and I knew I could be understood by her in a way that some of my family and friends are unable to grasp, through no fault of their own. It's the Mixed experience. Sherry Lee's voice, her story, will no doubt touch and heal many who read it."

> —Lola Osunkoya, MA Founder of Neither/Both LLC, Mixed-Race Community Building and Counseling

Critical Acclaim for Sherry Quan Lee's *Chinese Blackbird*

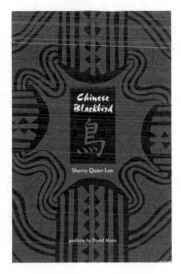

"Quan Lee eloquently expresses how painful and confusing it can be to embrace the many complex identities that one body can contain. With evocative imagery and words that cut straight to the heart, Quan Lee details her lifelong struggles with both the vagaries and concreteness of race, class, gender and sexual identity. Her guilt and shame are palpable. But so too are her emotional and intellectual triumphs. Like a favorite sad song when we have been dumped by the love of our lives, this volume will be oddly comforting to anyone who has ever been overcome by that sorrow which seems insurmountable."

—Edén Torres, Assistant Professor Women's Studies, Chicano Studies, University of Minnesota

"In *Chinese Blackbird*, Sherry Quan Lee renders stories of her complex cultural heritage with the lyrical touch of a poet coming into self-possession. Through the generative power of language, Lee creates an inspirational and a multifarious self. This self blows breath unto the page and into the reader, who may have felt quiescent or invisible, often feeling forced to choose among various enriching worlds, until she experiences the truth that only good literature can unveil about the joys and struggles of defining oneself on one's terms."

—-Pamela R. Fletcher, Associate Professor of English, Co-Director of Critical Studies in Race and Ethnicity, College of St. Catherine

CPSIA information can be obtained
at www.ICGtesting.com
Printed in the USA
FSHW021733090321
79307FS